BECOMING THE WAY WE ARE

An Introduction To Personal Development In Recovery And In Life

by Pamela Levin

Health Communications, Inc.
Deerfield Beach, Florida

First edition edited by Nora Gallagher
Second edition edited by Lori Baur
Third edition edited by Marie Stilkind and Paula Clodfelter

Library of Congress Cataloging in Publication Data
Levin, Pamela
  Becoming the Way We Are   84-070759

©1974, 1985, 1988 by Pamela Levin
First Edition Published 1974, Two Printings; Second Edition
Published 1984; Third Edition Published 1988.

ISBN 0-932194-84-2
Printed in the United States of America

Published by Health Communications, Inc.
        Enterprise Center
        3201 Southwest 15th Street
        Deerfield Beach, FL 33442

Dedication

TO THE CHILD
in everyone of
every age in
every stage

Thank You To

Eric Berne, who especially liked irreverent nurses

Claude Steiner, who made a challenge I could not refuse

Jacqui Schiff, who encouraged me to think *and* have needs

Ken Rashid for his powerful support and protection

My adventurous co-transformers and caretakers, who would rather live courageously than die in each moment

Laurie and Jon Weiss, who recognized significance in this material and provided their direct encouragements

Steve Karpman, who insisted that the material be written for all to share

Virginia Hilliker, who supported this risk-taking with her life and limb, who ate, slept and drank the theoretical constructs to assure their validity

My many new parents, who loved and nurtured me from birth to present and back again

Joan Menninger, who applied this material to the process of creative writing and then applied all that to me in loving form

Lloyd Linford and Jean Peters, who never failed support from the time of its conception on through labor and birth

Joe Concannon, my Clinical and Teaching sponsor, who never lost faith in my abilities, and so proved there really is a Santa Claus

Muriel James, Margaret Northcott, Peggy Love Tusler, Sheila Regan Coin, Emily Ruppert, Helen Colton, Pat Crossman and Peggy Cogswell for being strong, adequate and supportive women

Carla Haimowitz and Robert Mehler for their invaluable opinions, especially about this manuscript

Eleanor Regan, for her Herculean efforts, Zen typing skills and kind opinions

Loni Baur for her clarity and intelligent guidance with the second edition

Muriel Chapman, D.O., Jim Yensan, Shoshana Swartz and Jason Zimmet for their invaluable work with bodies and with mine in particular

Gail and Harold Nordeman for clear structure, complete commitment and loving constancy

Contents

Introduction

In which the witch hunts us, or we hunt the witch.

E.W.

All of us have "here and now" troubles. They may be money troubles, love troubles, hate troubles, sex troubles, boredom troubles, insignificant troubles or just plain nameless troubles, but troubles they are nonetheless. We all have them; they are part of being alive.

Some of us seem to have more troubles than others, or, at least, some of us seem to *feel* more troubles than others. Sometimes other people can see that we have more troubles than we need to have. Other people seem to know how not to have troubles which we can't seem to shake.

Sometimes current trouble is actually a part of our own personal history that we have allowed to continue to "cause trouble" in our lives long after the event has passed. If we have failed to integrate or resolve a childhood trauma or meet a need in the past, our current reality may become charged and contaminated, affecting our actions and experiences.

The past event can haunt and rehaunt us, becoming our own personal "witch". As a result we feel "not okay" — inadequate, unimportant, unlovely, unwhole or unholy. All our little hassles appear to be our total self. We are overwhelmed to the point where we feel like screaming.

This book is for people who want to make peace with their own personal history. It contains a summary of information which other travelers have found useful in their journey back from the old dungeons and demons of childhood.

The information on the following pages is a view of human growth and development using the tools of Transactional Analysis. The total picture is a composite made up of the experiences of many people who have traveled through their past in order to resolve it. All theoretical statements are based on my work with clients, observations of nature and my own personal growth. They are tools to aid, not replace, our inherent wisdom.

Part One describes the parts of our personality, our need for strokes, our tendency to play games and the scripts we advance as attempts to cope with issues. Alternatives are then presented for identifying those issues and transforming them by creating the protection we need to free ourselves from the limits of our scripts.

Part Two presents the Cycle of Development composed of six stages which begin in childhood and are repeated throughout our lives as a normal, natural process, part of the unfolding of life itself.

This booklet contains, then, a structure — a way of looking at the parts of our melodrama in order to see the whole. It is a map of the route, not the route itself. We who read the symbols must understand that words can only represent and not replace the spirit. The spirit is what we each provide.

PART ONE

BEGINNING

Get what you want to, if you want, 'cuz you can get anything.

Cat Stevens

The first step to getting what we want and need is often realizing that we *can* get it, that it's possible, available and that we deserve it. The beginning is starting to look at ourselves as we really are — unique and powerful beings.

We know from Eric Berne and the theories of Transactional Analysis[1], that within each of us grown-ups there are *three* unique aspects, or ego states, which give form to our completed personality structure: Parent, Adult and Child.

Parent   (P)   "I should"

Adult   (A)   "I think"

Child   (C)   "I feel, I need"

These three ego states function like three distinct beings within each one of us. For example, our Parent can judge and moralize: " You should do this, you shouldn't do that." Our Adult is our computer, our rational self, which can figure out practical solutions to problems using "data" from our experiences. Our Child can feel, need, dream, wish and have tantrums. Our Child is our source of creative energy.

Each of these facets of our being has its own voice which we can hear. If we feel pulled in several directions about a decision, our Parent might say, "You should *not* go to the beach today. It's utterly irresponsible!" Our Adult might say, "Today is Sunday. It's warm and sunny. The weather report is consistent with beach weather." Our Child might say, "I wanna go. I wanna. I wanna!"

A first step in looking at ourselves is *hearing* the voices within us and identifying them as Parent, Adult or Child so that we know who is speaking.

A second step involves *listening* to each voice so that we know "What is the message? Is it healthy? Does it lead to a resolution of the situation, or does it make matters worse? How is it affected by other messages? Is there a balance between them?" If our Child feels weak in the face of a strong Parental "You should!" it's goodbye to the beach for today, anyway, other options notwithstanding.

The decision to accept or reject messages from any of our ego states is often determined by one of the most powerful forces in life — our supply of strokes.

Activities For Beginning

Think of a decision you need to make and use it to complete the following sentences.

1. The voice of our Child ego state talks about feelings, wants and needs. For example:

   "I feel (mad, sad, happy, guilty, scared, delighted, etc.)."

   "I want (a new car, a vacation, a massage, a day in the sunshine, etc.)."

   "I need (a good night's sleep, more exercise, a good breakfast, etc.)."

   Now, complete the following sentences:

   My Child often feels _____
   My Child wants _____
   My Child needs _____

2. The voice of our Adult ego state is like a computer which reports thinking. For example, "I think (that 2 + 2 = 4, that the moon is almost full, that the traffic is less after sundown, that it is raining now, etc.)."

   Now, complete the following:

   My Adult thinks _____

3. The voice of our Parent ego state talks about values and morals. For example, "I should (finish this project, save my money, pay my taxes, exercise everyday, brush my teeth, etc.)."

   Now, complete the following:

   My Parent says I should _____

4. We may experience a conflict in an area of our lives such as following a diet, being on time for appointments, spending money.
   Use this exercise as an example:

   My Parent says, "I should exercise every day."

   My Adult reports these facts: "It is possible to do; other people do it."

   "I am a busy person."

   "The information about how to do it is available."

   My Child says, "I wanna play. I'm tired. Reading this novel is more fun."

Now, complete the following:

An area of my life in which I experience a conflict is: _____
_____

In regard to this conflict:

   My Child often feels _____

   My Adult thinks _____

   My Parent says I should _____
   _____

What I will do is _____
_____

STROKES

In which we try or die . . .

Many of us may have fooled ourselves into believing that life is just one disappointment after another, that there is no light at the end of the tunnel and that maybe there isn't even a tunnel! On the other hand, we may believe people who say, "All you have to do is think positively and brush your teeth everyday and everything will turn out all right."

Occasionally, though, we may see something different. We may spend a few hours giggling with a friend just like kids. Someone may have said something so endearing and funny that we reached over and hugged them. Or perhaps a friend said, "You look wonderful!"

Some of us were taught to believe that these messages were too insignificant to make a difference in our lives. It is, however, these very same messages that can connect us to our high and energetic spaces. Lacking them, we feel unloved and physically depressed. Accepting affectionate, affirming exchanges with others, we no longer keep ourselves down.

Babies need strokes as much as they need food. If they don't get strokes, ultimately they will die.[2] Babies need to be patted and cuddled. Children need to be touched and loved because strokes are an essential source of fuel, just as food is a source of energy. Children who get too little stroking become disinterested in their surroundings and withdraw from the world.

Grown-ups are no different from babies in this respect. We all need a supply of food to keep our bodies functioning and healthy. We also need stroking. We need to be touched, recognized, gentled. Just as other animals have their grooming rituals, so we have our stroking rules and rituals. We are often careful not to make any choices that adversely affect our supply of strokes. Our behavior is determined by what we feel we can afford — a supply and demand of strokes.

We can learn a great deal about how we run our lives, or how our lives run us, by examining our past with strokes in mind. If we think about it, we can see in which exchanges with others we felt high and energetic, and in which ones we felt sad, and how our choices were affected by our stroke supply.

We can identify the rules by which we seek our strokes. Some of us were taught that we can't ask for strokes, or, even worse, that we shouldn't need them. Children often run into a room, crawl into a lap and ask for a hug, but adults behaving in such a way infringe on social rules and risk being cut off from further stroking.

However, believing that we can't ask for strokes doesn't change the fact that we need them. When we believe we are only allowed the needs that are "on the menu" for the day, and strokes are not listed, we are in a quandary. Should we change the menu? Should we go underground instead, seeking what we need indirectly by playing a *game* (discussed in the next chapter)?

Activities for Strokes

My favorite strokes I like to give to myself are:

1. _____
2. _____
3. _____
4. _____
5. _____

The strokes I like to give others are:

1. _____
2. _____
3. _____
4. _____
5. _____

The strokes I like to receive from others are:

1. _____
2. _____
3. _____
4. _____
5. _____

Strokes I decided never to accept no matter how badly I may
want or need them are:

1. _____

2. _____

3. _____

4. _____

5. _____

GAMES³

Goin' fishin', instead of just a wishin' . . .

If we don't ask for what we need directly and if we don't want to starve, we can go "a fishin'". We spend our psychic energy playing games in an attempt to get our needs met indirectly. If we are clever and dedicated, we can manipulate the situation so that what we are fishing for takes the bait and we can feel as if we have won. However, playing games ultimately leads to deprivation because it takes more energy than it returns. It takes more energy to reach a goal by an indirect route than by a direct one. In other words, it takes more energy to be passive about a problem than to be active about it.

When we deplete or dam up our reserves of energy we are, in effect, starving ourselves. Our energy is either gone or unavailable, and we feel even more needy. We may decide to play another, harder game to "up the ante", hoping for a better return. This is called "escalation".

Escalation is the process by which we wall off or drain psychic energy in an attempt to render it inactive. Four types of behavior signal escalation. Each can follow the other in a step-like progression unless we reverse the process.

The Four Passive Behaviors[4]

1. Doing nothing (relevant to the problem)
2. Over-adapting (doing what someone else's Parent says to do, instead of doing what we need to do)
3. Agitating (becoming emotionally disturbed, tremulous)
4. Incapacitation or violence (imploding, that is, going crazy, or exploding, hitting someone)

If we fail to ask for what we need directly, we can choose our kind of escalation from the many varieties of games. Our game choice in a particular situation is often determined by how many strokes we can get. Usually the larger the potential stroke yield, the more attractive the game. However, since our position is that we can't get what we need, we set up the situation so that we get only what we think is available — negative strokes. These are some examples:

- We run ourselves down whenever someone compliments us.
- We pick a fight for no apparent reason.
- We act increasingly incompetent until someone reacts negatively to us.
- We fuss about others' actions until we feel justified in raging about their incompetence.

Many of us go through our lives asking for and getting negative strokes. We become more and more unhappy and unable to change things. We expect bad things to happen to us, and we act out the same scenes again and again with the same results. This kind of "set" behavior is often the result of a problem started long ago in our childhood, when negative strokes were the only kind of recognition we could safely receive. The "set" or pattern has become part of our *script*.

Activities for Games

Feeling bad is an indication that we may be involved in a game. The bad feelings I often have are:

1. _____

2. _____

3. _____

4. _____

For each feeling listed above, write below the limiting belief that led to this feeling. For example:

Feeling	Belief
a. boredom	a. I can't get the pleasurable stimulation I need.
b. sadness	b. Life is one loss after another.
c. guilt	c. If I make my own choices, I will suffer the consequences.

Now, complete the following:

Feeling	Belief
1. _____	1. _____
2. _____	2. _____
3. _____	3. _____
4. _____	4. _____

Now, consider how much longer you want to continue reinforcing limiting beliefs instead of getting what you need. For each belief listed above, write down the kind of reinforcement you really need and want, as in the following example:

Limiting Belief

a. I can't get the pleasurable stimulation I need.

b. My life is one loss after another.

c. If I make my own choices I will suffer the consequences.

What I Need to Know

a. I can get all the protection and support I need to explore my world safely.

b. People care about me and will stick around; I can rely on others to be there for me.

c. The more I actively and freely make my own choices, the more I benefit myself and those around me.

Now, complete the following:

Limiting Belief	What I Need to Know
1. _____	1. _____
2. _____	2. _____
3. _____	3. _____
4. _____	4. _____

SCRIPTS[5]

For the sins of the fathers shall be visited upon the sons for generations unto generations of them that hate me.

Holy Bible

We record our entire personal history in our ego states.
The way we were as children doesn't go away when we get
older. It remains a dynamic part of us, motivating our current
experiences. If we didn't get what we needed as children, we
continue to seek it symbolically through dramatic scenes
enacted in the here-and-now. The scenes are taken from our
"script", our personal story or collection of early decisions
and unmet needs, now long forgotten. We continue to use
them to program our current experiences, even without
being aware of them. Scripts represent our attempts to get
needs met which were not met originally. When we play out
our script as grown-ups, we act in ways which are symbolic of
the original unsatisfactory childhood experience. Thus, script
behavior is predetermined. We are controlled by yesterday,
as if we were haunted by demons or hunted by witches. We
are just the opposite of spontaneous, autonomous, creative
beings. Prisoners of our past, we are not free to live today.

Most of us didn't get everything we needed as we were
growing up, and so most of us have scripts. We are attached
to some aspects of our personal history in the present
moment. Using script programs we structure our time by
symbolically attempting to meet the needs we had yesterday
or yesteryear. These symbolic efforts don't work, however,
because they suffer from bad timing. Still, we may continue
the same unrewarding and repetitious patterns because our
needs remain unmet.

Although there are many varieties of script programs, they
all function to make us seem some other way than we really
are. Each particular illusion is one we decided to assume as
we were growing up in order to get the caring that was
available. Here are two of the most common illusions:

Stay Little
(Don't Grow Up)

Our parents may not have said,
"Stay little." They may have
been afraid of our growing up
and leaving them with nothing
to do.

Hurry and Grow Up
(Don't Be Dependent)

Our parents may not have said,
"Don't be little." They may
have feared close contact and
dependency.

Stay Little (Don't Grow Up)	Hurry and Grow Up (Don't Be Dependent)
The way we get strokes is to look little and inadequate.	The way we get strokes is by acting threatening.
We act as if the only way to do things is to get someone else to do them for us.	We act as if the only way to do things is to do them our way only.
We try to keep close to people.	We try to keep people at a distance.
We are controlled by the space around us.	We control the space around us.
We diminish our awareness to look impotent.	We heighten our awareness to look powerful.
We try to "kill time".	We try to "make time".
We have trouble making up our minds, often waiting for someone else to make them up for us.	We point out other people's faults a lot. We are among the first to notice others' imperfections.
We rarely get mad and often act scared instead.	We rarely get scared. We deny our fear and get mad instead.
We agree with people often, no matter what they are saying, unless they say, "Disagree!"	We act in opposition to most situations; we don't often agree with others.
We try to anticipate what others need before they ask.	We are afraid to let other people know we have needs.
We take care of other people, even when we don't feel like it.	We are afraid to take care of other people because we feel we'll get "milked dry".

The beginning of getting out of our script is recognizing that we are in it. Recognition is the first step. The second step is identifying the need which our script attempts to meet, however unsuccessfully. We have then started to let go of yesterday's pain and be alive today.

Activities for Scripts

1. Return to the lists on p. 17 and check each aspect that applies to you.

2. Think of the child you once were. Who is the older friend or relative that child most closely identified with?

   _____

3. Describe in a sentence or two:

   a. The positive aspects of that person's life.

   _____

   b. The negative aspects. _____

   _____

4. Think about your life now. In what ways are you following a life pattern similar to this person? _____

   _____

   _____

5. Think for a moment about any negative or harmful patterns you still play out in your current life. If you continue on your present course, where will you be:

   In 5 years: _____
   In 10 years: _____
   In 20 years: _____

6. What do you need to do now to turn that negative script payoff into a positive desirable one? _____

   _____

   _____

IDENTIFYING
PROBLEMS

All that we have ever been and all that we ever need to be is known in the eternal place inside ourselves where all is quiet.

Ram Dass[6]

One of the most important steps we can take in working through a script problem is deciding that we can stand what we are feeling. When we keep ourselves locked into limiting or destructive script behavior, it is because our Child is still responding to a feeling as if it were a real and present danger. Actually, though, the feeling of danger is archaic. Archaic feelings are those that were once dangerous to express because they might upset the family equilibrium. When we decide as adults to get in touch with and be aware of these feelings, our internal Child often feels like we are going to destroy the family or its current equivalent — our friends or groups. In fact, we are merely re-experiencing a previous danger. The feeling of danger is part of our old program, an illusion carried over from yesteryear.

A second step in moving beyond script illusions is dealing with feeling fragile. We continue to feel fragile and impotent as adults because as children we gave up our power in the original situation in order to maintain stability. Again, this is part of our old script illusion, our archaic feelings. It is not part of our current reality.

Deciding to stand what we are feeling and dealing with being fragile, then, are two aids to keeping the illusion in clearer perspective. We see it for what it is — just an old piece of unfinished business, and we see ourselves for who we are — powerful and capable.

Writing down the information about a problem that we become aware of is often beneficial. Picking up paper and pencil can aid our thinking, our Adult computer processes. Identifying a script issue is just that process — deciding to think about it.

We can structure our way of thinking about a problem and put the parts together in order to see the whole. The following structure is a way to see any script issue as a total picture:

Think Structure[7]

I am _____
    (feeling)

because I think that if I _____
                        (behavior I initiate)

I will be _____
          (unhealthy Parental response)

instead of _____
           (healthy Parental response)

so I _____
    (problem justifying behaviors, games)

Identifying a script issue is always a process of trial and error. We may need to change things in the blanks several times as we focus our feelings and can tell more accurately what feels right.

The clearest picture results when we use the words of a five-year-old for feelings such as "scared, mad, sad and glad", and when we are specific about what behavior the feeling generates. Our behavior offers accurate clues as to the archaic age of our problems.

Examples of identified archaic problems using this particular structure may look like this:

I am ___scared_____
    (feeling)

because I think that if I ___cry to be held____
                        (behavior I initiate)

I will be ___beaten_____
          (unhealthy Parental response)

instead of ___nurtured_____
           (healthy Parental response)

so I ___act cute and coy when I need_____

_____something, wait to ask until I can't stand it,___

_____
drink to numb the need, smoke and eat
(problem justifying behavior)

I am ___angry_____
(feeling)

because I think that if I ___show any angry behavior at all___
(behavior I initiate)

I will be ___abandoned by my parents who will get sick___

___and hysterical_____
(unhealthy Parental response)

instead of ___their dealing with my anger___
(healthy Parental response)

so I ___act scared, helpless, weak and fragile, and___
do what others want me to do
(problem justifying behavior)

Activities for Identifying Problems

1. Think about a problem you are experiencing in your current life. Fill out the following Think Structure:

I feel _____
(feeling)

because I think that if I _____
(behavior I initiate)

I will be _____
(unhealthy Parental response)

instead of _____
(healthy Parental response)

so I _____
(problem justifying behavior, games)

2. Reread the sentence you have just completed in 1. Allowing yourself to be creative, and without censoring any idea, no matter how absurd or impossible, list all the things you might do about it. (For example, one person who completed a Think Structure about money worries made this list: see a therapist, skip town, refuse to pay any of my bills, insist that someone else handle it, borrow money, regress to an age too young to be expected to deal with it, consult with an accountant, pay part of each bill, pay all of some bills and delay payment on others.)

   a. _____

   b. _____

   c. _____

   d. _____

   e. _____

   f. _____

   g. _____

   h. _____

   i. _____

3. Without *thinking* about it, write down how old the child in you feels when you experience the problem you identified above.

   I feel _____ (months, years) old

Use this age as a reference in choosing which chapter to read in order to learn about the dynamics, tasks and process of resolution consistent with that age.

TRANSFORMATION

Remember, misery is optional.
Joan Menninger

Transformation occurs when we get what we need and thus let go of a piece of personal history. When we let go, we allow the archaic memory to have as much energy as we need for a resolution. We let our feelings run the show.

All the information we need about our childhood programming exists in our feelings. Our feelings tell us exactly what happened and what we need to do. They are part of our original "recording" of a situation, and provide access to further information so that we can arrive at the total picture. If we remain aware of our feelings and give them full attention, we can determine what we need in order to resolve them. We can then tear down the wall between our current selves and our basic sanity. This process is called Transformation. The word "transform" means to change in structure, form, condition, nature or character. The image is one of a metamorphosis as when the caterpillar enters its cocoon only to leave it as a butterfly. When we change the nature of an archaic limitation, we emerge supported by that which had previously limited us.

We can release ourselves from script limitations regardless of whether they were made the day we were born, weaned, toilet trained, punished for truancy or had our first date. We can re-enter the early memory and remove the energy, the "charge" from the original experience. We replace the old destructive program with a new, constructive one.

In this way, we transform limitations acquired since birth. If our original experience led us to the decision that we have no right to exist, we can reenter that experience, discharge the dammed-up energy, and create a new experience from which we emerge with full support for our right to exist.

During our childhood we develop programs at different ages as we build the machinery of our personality. The programs function in our grown-up life, just as the automatic pilot functions in an airplane. If our programming is faulty, we may have a rough flight or even a crash landing. If the equipment is not damaged beyond repair, we can redesign the program to support the machinery of our personalities and bodies.

Reprogramming requires us to become temporarily the child we once were in order that the child can have new experiences from which to create a new program. For successful reprogramming we need external support, contact with others, in order to maintain our connection to reality and prevent us from getting stuck in self-destructive spaces.

Since most destructive programs at least infer that some aspect of our self is crazy, we often feel as if we were about to go crazy as we venture closer to a solution. If we have spent our lives up until now perched on a powder keg of archaic rage, we have no doubt been careful not to light any emotional matches. Our decision to create protection for letting that anger take over and run us for a while will probably not be made without some resistance. A wee small voice inside us may object, "No, no! I'll kill somebody," or "No, no! Somebody will kill me!"

This is a good time to remember that whether we live out of our collection of illusions or out of our basic sanity is our choice, our decision. If we don't keep this fact in mind, we may prevent ourselves from problem-solving in order to avoid experiencing this often intense fear of going crazy. When we are ready to enter an old progam, we are in a good position to remake that decision. The outcome of our journey depends on whether we want to resolve it or to stay in it. It is our decision alone.

Activities for Transformation

1. Feeling "crazy" is a response to an experience which we believe is not okay or is abnormal. From the following list, circle the feelings or experiences that you learned were "not okay", bad or abnormal. Complete the list by adding any other words which apply to you.

   Joyful, sad, tired, grieved, proud, energetic, sexy, doubtful, mad, jealous, aggressive, glad, scared, hungry, timid, full.

   Other: _____

2. For each item you circled in 1., describe what you do to avoid having that experience. For example:

Instead of feeling *mad,* I *get scared.*
Instead of feeling *scared,* I *get busy doing things.*

Instead of feeling _____ I _____
Instead of feeling _____ I _____
Instead of feeling _____ I _____
Instead of feeling _____ I _____
Instead of feeling _____ I _____

3. Now read the list again. This time, next to each item you circled, place a number on a scale of 1 to 10 to denote the level of resistance you feel about allowing yourself to feel this experience, with number 1 being the lowest and 10 being the highest. This number represents the degree of protection you may need to arrange for the transformation which will allow the experience to be okay, healthy and normal again.

PROTECTION[8]

Why, you're nothing but a pack of cards!
Alice, in *Alice in Wonderland*

When we create protection for ourselves, we clear the path ahead so that we can feel whatever we feel and stay conscious in the face of those feelings. Protection is the key with which we can open up the door to our vast storehouse of past experiences. Protection is essential on our journey into these spaces because they are beyond the influence of the usual states of consciousness which contain our counterscript.

A counterscript is a collection of methods we have learned to use to neutralize temporarily or to "counter" our destructive script. Protection provides an external environment in which we can not only prevent danger, but also permanently resolve the script.

When we feel protected, we experience that there is no immediate danger of injury or loss which will result from our facing or helping someone else to face an archaic event.

There is no specific formula for protection, but as we set up protection in each situation we can keep in mind three important points:

1. We need protection given to us in a form specific to the age of the inner Child who made the script decision. If the decision was made in our teenage years, we can receive others' compassion through words. That same compassion must be translated into direct physical contact to connect with our inner Child who is younger than words.

2. To feel protected enough to work through script issues successfully, we require right here and now one or more caring competent people. We need to feel secure enough to let out a Child who may be scared, sad, angry or hurting. To make sure others' support is real and not just talk, we need to grant them the right to say no to anything they may not want to do. Such protection contributes to a successful outcome because their discomfort sheds new light on the entire situation.

3. We create protection with others by making a contract. The contract is the vehicle through which we give and receive protection.[9] In adult language a contract is a

legal, mutual agreement entered into by one or more competent parties. It states clearly what each person wants from the relationship and what each person is going to give. In Child words, a contract creates safe methods for giving and receiving love.

We can make profound changes when we focus our external relationships in this way. First we become aware that a present destructive pattern is a repetition of an earlier traumatic experience. Then by arranging the protection we need to resolve the earlier experience, we create a new experience which by its very existence has begun to replace the original one. We feel safer and stronger as each moment passes.

Activities for Protection

1. When I think about arranging protection for the little girl or boy inside of me, I feel:

   _____

2. The little girl or boy inside me needs protection from (circle those that apply):
   a. Being physically hurt
   b. Being emotionally hurt
   c. Being criticized
   d. Being blamed
   e. Having to take care of others by growing up too fast
   f. Having to take care of others by not growing up
   g. Being abandoned
   h. Being unloved
   i. Feeling unworthy

Include items circled above when you make a contract with others for protection.

A Setting For
"GOING SANE"

People with belly buttons are allowed 20% error.
Barbara Miller

The information about transforming programs from developmental stages in our childhood comes from several sources. The original work came from the experiences of many seriously disturbed young people who had been adopted by Jacqui and Moe Schiff. These "children" underwent regression, staying little and growing up again, and resolved developmental problems in a process called *reparenting.*

Ten years and many groups later, we have more information, new revelations, and a new process called *corrective parenting,* based on the experiences of thousands of people. Now, when we need to work something through, we use this information in ongoing groups. The same eight to ten people meet once a week for a period of time ranging from a few months to a year or so. Some people attend weekend marathons in addition. Some simply call together a group of experienced friends when they need to work something through in a "one shot deal".

The atmosphere at such meetings is informal, relaxed and personal. People physically stroke each other and visit as they settle down into a pleasant, shared experience. The room used for the meeting is a place where it is safe for grown-ups to be little. Typically, it is arranged with a large mattress on the floor for people to sit or lie on, and an enormous number of pillows — the more the better. There are several baby bottles with crosscut nipples, some baby food and a good supply of milk, juice, cookies, crackers and teething biscuits. There are toys of various kinds which a grown-up child can safely rattle, bang, bite or throw. There are usually pacifiers and teething rings which have been safely selected to withstand the strength of a grown-up toddler's bite.

The meeting is scheduled with enough time so that people do not have to feel hurried in what they need to do. People are on time because lateness interrupts the flow of group energy (unless it is prearranged). Everyone wears comfortable, loose clothing and people often take their shoes off and sit close together on the mattress and pillows. At the beginning anyone who wants to work states what he or she needs to do. Then the entire group decides what the group will invest its time in doing first. It is essential for a good reprogramming experience that every person's needs be included right from the beginning.

The person whose turn it is to work offers a brief description of the work he or she wishes to do. This usually includes information about the feeling and what it wants to do, the age of feeling and the nature of a resolution.

"I have a pain in my stomach. I think I've been swallowing anger most of my life. I think it's young because I feel wobbly when I let the feeling rise, and I have pain in my teeth, maybe teething pain. I will probably need you to give me something to bite. I think I had to give up stroking when I was active. That's probably why I'm angry. I want a lot of stroking from people, especially when I feel active. That's how I'll know I don't have to give up other needs in order to *do* things."

Anything unclear is clarified and any objections to what is being set up are dealt with. In addition, a method of stopping (if need be) is arranged. After the leader is assured that everyone is ready, the person is usually told, "Go ahead and let the feeling take over and do what you need to do."

So far there have not been any needs that are actually unmeetable. There have been no archaic problems that have turned out to be unsolvable. No piece of suffering has been so large or severe or scary that it could not be released or resolved. People have been able to look at the facts and say, "I can solve it; it is solvable."[10]

Activities for "Going Sane"

1. With regard to the problem I want to resolve, I am feeling _____

2. I feel this in my body (describe where you feel it) ___
   _____

3. I feel _____ (months, years) old

4. What I do not want you to do is _____

_____

(Examples: Leave me, criticize me, tell me to be quiet, etc.)

5. What I know so far about what I will want you to do is

_____

_____

(Examples: Touch my head, tell me it's okay to scream, give me a pillow to hit, hold me close, etc.)

6. When I resolve this, what I will be able to have or do in my life is (describe):

_____

_____

_____

The following section contains a summary of the Six Stages of the Developmental Cycle, including information and exercises useful in identifying and working through script issues.

PART TWO

The
DEVELOPMENTAL
CYCLE

*All movements are accomplished in six stages and
the seventh brings return. Thus the winter solstice,
with which the decline of the year begins, comes in
the seventh month after the summer solstice . . . In
this way the state of rest gives place to movement.*
                    I-Ching, Book of Changes

Nature's pattern of growth is cyclic. This can be seen in the planets, as they move in orbit, only to return to the place from which they started. It can be observed in the course of the sun and moon through the sky, in the seasons of the year, in the continuing cycle of plant and animal life.

As a part of nature, we, too, pass through stages in our development. This cyclical evolution means that we return to certain issues and themes over the course of time as we pass, and repass through the stages:

Stage One:	Being
Stage Two:	Doing
Stage Three:	Thinking
Stage Four:	Identity
Stage Five:	Skillfulness
Stage Six:	Regeneration
Stage Seven:	Recycling

As we pass through each stage in childhood, we have an opportunity to become familiar with the developmental design. We can develop a basic power of ability in each stage as our situation requires.

When we repeat the stages in adulthood, we have a chance to refine and further develop this power by carrying out developmental tasks associated with each stage. In this way, we align ourselves with the cyclic process of nature and claim the capacities which are inherently ours.

The following pages provide a description, a summary, and a set of exercises for each stage. By discovering our developmental design, we can maximize our potential for growth, health and satisfaction as we continue our endless journey through the cycle.

STAGE ONE

BEING

The Natural Child
(Birth to Six Months)

To be or not to be, that is the question.
                                    Shakespeare

The events of the first six months of our lives are crucial to all the rest of our development. The way we experience our existence for the rest of our lives is largely determined by the foundation we create while we are still helpless. Our first basic "set" or program is the building block upon which we support all our later developmental experiences and decisions. This is our basic position in life, our okay-ness, and our right to be taking up space in the physical plane. It is our basic existential position.

All the experiences from which we derive our first program are recorded in ego states we call the Natural Child. They are on film and on file in each of us, a personal documentary of how we each arrived at our basic life position. They are represented in our dreams by floating-feeling-formless-misty images which are filled with high pleasurable sensations or ghouls, monsters, sadistic attackers and unknown dangers, depending upon our early life experiences.

During our first months we are completely helpless physically. We can only kick and flail aimlessly except for one purposeful behavior — our ability to cry. Crying is our first stimulus, our first attempt to communicate with the rest of the world. It is our first ability to be adequate. The response of the environment to our cry completes our first transaction.

Our relationship to our environment is our umbilical cord to life because we are not capable of thinking or carrying out complicated tasks. We depend on borrowing these capacities from others through a relationship called symbiosis. Transactionally, a symbiotic relationship is one in which the functions of feeling, thinking and doing are shared between two or more people. Our first program is the result of our transactions in this relationship.

We reach conclusions about what life is like based on transactions around two basic needs — feeding and stroking. Taking in food, we stimulate and define our innermost physical boundary or gut. Taking in strokes through touch, we define our outermost boundary or skin. In addition to supplying fuel for a rapidly growing body, in meeting these needs we experience that we exist physically and that we are real. We also discover where our own body stops and the rest of the world begins.

If we are required to wait time after time when we signal that our fuel supply is low, we may decide that our existence is not important, or that we are not to be trusted about our needs. Later we may not recognize that we need something until our blood sugar is dangerously low and our spinal nerves are vibrating with pain. Conversely, if the grown-ups taking care of us were over-anxious, they may have anticipated what we needed, thereby preventing us from developing the capacity to organize the sea of sensations in our bodies in such a way that we can *know* that we need something, let alone know *what* we need. If early experiences were painful, we can know that we may act powerful, strong, angry, hard and cold as adults as a way of protecting our scared, hungry, needy-baby feelings.

When we set up a reprogramming situation in the presence of an effective, affectionate caretaker, we need to use only those channels which an actual infant has available because these are the body systems in which we need to record the experience. In this way we can record a new program and get a new "take" on an old scene. We become physically helpless again. We may not be able to hold ourselves up in a sitting position. Reflexes become our only behavioral activity. We cannot create our new experience of satisfaction by looking at pictures of milk; we need the real experience — being hungry and getting fed.

We cannot digest words that tell us how cute we are, but we can create a new program from the only kind of love an infant can know — gentle touching from people who care. When we experience being totally taken care of in a loving way by those around us, we have the experience we need to change our first, limiting decisions and create a new life position. Now we can be glad we are alive. We can decide that we are indeed a Child of the universe. We can choose to experience the truth.

Summary

Ego state: Natural Child

Developmental age: Birth to six months

Activity: Needs and feelings

Functional metaphor: Generator

Psychoanalytic
equivalent: Early Oral

Needs: Feeding and stroking, imme-
                            diate response to crying sig-
                            nal

Key concepts: Adequacy, supply, using
                            anger to cover fear, basic
                            existential position, depen-
                            dency, helplessness

Common body
problems: Disturbances in the sustain-
                            ing systems (those without
                            which life cannot continue);
                            immunologic (susceptibility
                            to infections); digestive (in-
                            ability to digest foods, ulcers,
                            inflammations); eliminative
                            (constipation, diarrhea); cir-
                            culatory (impaired circula-
                            tion, high or low blood pres-
                            sure); respiratory (wheezing,
                            lowered lung capacity, pneu-
                            monia, bronchitis); nervous
                            irritability (hypo or hyper
                            reflexes, numbness); blocked
                            genital feelings

Problem-solving
procedure: Peek-a-boo

Games and positions: NIGYSOB (Now I got you, you
                            SOB), obesity, bag-o-bones,
                            addict, indigent, chain smoker

Mechanism:	Denial
Injunctions, set-ups:	Don't be, don't feel, don't have needs
Messages in support of *Being*:	It's okay for you to be here, to be fed, touched and taken care of. You have a right to be here. Your needs are okay with me. I'm glad you're a (boy/girl). I like to hold you, to be near you, to touch you. You don't have to hurry, you can take your time.

Activities for Stage One

1. I know when I need to be taken care of for a while because I:

_____ am tired   _____ do more and more tasks
_____ am irritable   _____ eat
_____ am depressed   _____ starve
_____ am nervous   _____ think a lot
_____ need more sleep   _____ have trouble sleeping
_____ can't sleep   other _____

2. When I imagine myself in my life now being taken care of exactly as I want and need, the following scene comes to mind:

_____

_____

_____

_____

3. When I picture the baby I once was and who remains an active, vital part of my life, I feel:

_____ scared, _____ sad, _____ happy, _____ joyous, _____ depressed, _____ enraged, _____ panicked

other _____

4. What the baby I once was needs to know and hear right now is:

_____

_____

5. I will give and receive the messages in support of *Being* to myself and others in the following ways:

_____

_____

_____

STAGE TWO

DOING

The Little Professor
(Six Months to Eighteen Months)

Don't tame the Wild God.

Chogyam Trungpa

When we work through problems from the ages of around six months to eighteen months, we are beginning to bridge the gap between the symbiosis with parents and doing things on our own. Although we still borrow the functions of thinking and doing from our dependency relationship, we begin to initiate transactions by means other than crying. Our bodies are well developed enough to sit up, and later, to crawl toward sources of stimulation, to pick up objects and to taste, touch, smell, see and hear sources of energy, much like a radar screen scans the environment in search of sources of stimulation.

This new need to explore the environment in search of sensory experience is a new capacity developing which Transactional Analysis calls the Little Professor. It stretched out from the earlier dependency of the Natural Child like a sprout from a new leaf.

But just as a new leaf withers when it does not receive enough energy to supply it, these new capacities also wither in people who have to sacrifice their Natural Child needs in order to explore. Not being able to explore to a baby this age is like being asked to starve. If someone in the environment expects us to inhibit our behavior in a certain area ("Don't touch that vase! No, no, leave that alone!"), we may choose to inhibit all behavior. Since we are too young to limit behavior selectively, we may decide to become passive.

The net effect of many such repeated experiences is that we undercut our motivation. Having made this choice in childhood, we may experience little or no interest in doing things (especially new things) as adults. Our adult behavior is ritualized, listless and lifeless. We have replaced fascination with depression. Or we may have discovered that in our original exploratory experiences we decided that the only way to get attention was to escalate activity. Consequently, we engage in certain behaviors which are as varied as human imagination. Instead of devoting ourselves to creating the affection and safe exploration we need to feed and satisfy our curiosity, we devote ourselves to become a "star", or perhaps to excelling at intellectual pursuits in order to get needs met.

(This may have been our prejudice when this ego state was named the Little Professor.)

We may act stupid or sick to get protection and strokes. Some of us may even act constantly happy, or always tough or fragile. Some of us may decide always to be doing something. In our adult lives, we are all stuck with our "trick", believing it is the only way to get our needs met. If our trick is to do intellectual magic acts, we become more and more heady until we finally drive ourselves to collapse. This set-up is particularly insidious because many of us have become so expert at our trick, that our escalation looks like a flash of brilliance or a good feeling while inside we are feeling more and more pain.

What we need to do is to take in energy through our senses that is essential to the development of our physical body and of our voluntary nervous system. When we are deprived of this energy or are only allowed to explore it when we do tricks, we find that we have behavioral problems, perceptual problems and motivational problems. They range from the silly — "I can't hear with my glasses off!" to the serious — sight, hearing and speech difficulties.

The effects of unmet exploratory needs show up in adult behavior as gawkiness, awkwardness or a spastic quality to movements. Blocks in doing things seem to produce physical stress reaction as if adrenal glands were stuck producing vast amounts of adrenalin. Physically and psychologically we seem "stuck" in one of the self-preservation reactions — fight, flight or freeze.[11]

In some of us a stroke hunger from the previous six months coupled with a stress reaction from this stage results in the symptoms of asthma.

Solving problems from this stage always seems easier than identifying them. We need to have protective, affectionate caretaking, feeding and stroking while we follow the impulses of our "radar". If we come to a dangerous situation, we want to be offered two "yeses" instead of only a "no". ("You can't bite the lamp cord. Here's a cracker or your teething ring.") Once it is safe for us to follow our noses, we heal our physical difficulties easily. If we no longer have to inhibit all behavior, we easily become spontaneous, creative and motivated. We may report that if we no longer have to pull energy in through our eyes only, our vision improves.

We experience the protection necessary to do this when we know there is no requirement for us to behave in any one way. We can do what we want to do, including nothing, and we will still be protected. We can still get feeding and stroking. We don't have to sacrifice comfort for growth. We know that our caretakers will always offer options[12] (yeses) instead of inhibitions (no's).

Summary

Ego state: Little Professor

Developmental age: Six to eighteen months

Activity: Behavior

Functional metaphor: Radar

Psychoanalytic equivalent: Oral exploratory

Needs: Exploring and doing things, two "yeses" for every "no"

Key concepts: Initiating, motivation, curiosity, creativity, intuition, motion, exploring, options, grounding, using fear to cover anger

Common body problems: Adrenal stress reaction activated with behavior stuck in flight, fight or freeze response; sensory motor impairments (hypo or hyper activity); perceptual problems, visual, auditory; asthma; migraine

Problem-solving procedure: You'll never get away

Games and positions:	Do me something, cavalier, sweetheart, me too, harried, asthma, gee, you're wonderful, greenhouse
Mechanism:	Projection
Injunctions, set-ups:	Don't bother (me); don't initiate; don't do things; don't be curious, real, intuitive
Messages in support of *Doing*:	It's okay for you to move out in the world, to explore, to feed your senses and be taken care of. It's okay for you to explore and experiment. You can do things and get support at the same time. It's okay for you to initiate. You can be curious and intuitive. You can get attention or approval and still act the way you really feel.

Activities for Stage Two

1. I know when I need to explore the possibilities of my life or my environment because:

_____ I am restless   _____ my production goes way down

_____ I am bored   _____ my motivation diminishes

_____ my concentration is short   _____ I need to move, see, hear new places, people and things

_____ my attention wanders   _____ thinking about what to do doesn't work

2. When I imagine myself in my life now having the freedom, safety and affection I need to explore exactly as I want and need, the following scene comes to mind:

_____

_____

_____

_____

3. When I picture the toddler I once was who is still an active vital part of my life, I feel:

_____ scared, _____ sad, _____ happy, _____ joyous,
_____ depressed, _____ enraged, _____ panicked
other _____

4. What that toddler I once was needs to know and hear right now is:

_____

_____

5. I will give and receive new messages about *Doing* to myself in the following ways:

_____

_____

_____

_____

STAGE THREE

THINKING

The Adult Ego State
(Eighteen Months to Three Years)

No, I won't, and you can't make me.
                                    Anonymous

When we get in touch with problems in getting our needs met between the ages of about eighteen months to three years, we report feeling "stuck" and confused. Questions about our experience are usually answered, "I don't know." We report feeling extremely uncomfortable, often tired and "muddy". Attempts by others to interpret this turn of events never work out. In fact, when others think for us, the problem intensifies. We get more stuck. Soon everyone is puzzled and more than a few are angry. It looks like a terminal case of resistance.

Although we don't give others any direct answers during the time we are locked into that experience, we may be "learning to think". We are gaining the ability to use our own "computer". The long pauses, which puzzle and anger others and which they often interpret as resistance, are indications that we are putting some order into our sea of sensory experiences. We are developing the ability to "remember" at will, thus gaining the capacity to make connections between two or more sensory events. While others are waiting, we are integrating.

Those of us who had information withheld from us at this age may feel that our capacity to think and know has been discounted, that is, not taken into account. Our thinking was undercut because, without certain information, we could not adequately assess our needs and feelings. It's hard to prepare for the stimulation of a grocery store when we don't know where we are going until we get there.

We may feel there is a conspiracy afoot to keep us uninformed. As grown-ups, we may become angry and controlling, and stubbornly maintain a position, even if we have made up our minds arbitrarily. This behavior seems to result from being made to feel that dependency is not safe. We may appear little and helpless, take hours to make up our minds and then change them, preferring to control the situation from that position. This results from feeling that independence is not safe.

Often we push others for the information we need only to have them control the situation for us. Our pushing then turns to rage. If we try a thought-out approach, asking questions, others may become enraged with *us,* reversing the positions of parent and child in the symbiosis so that the one who needs parental care becomes the one who takes care of the parents by thinking for them. All of these strategies interfere with the natural ordering of our new ego state, the Adult computer. We may develop messy or very tidy habits. We fend off any external order with a stubborn, "I won't," usually cleverly masked behind heightened or diminished consciousness and behavior — acting smart or stupid.

We need enough time, enough space, enough strokes, enough information and a loving attitude from others while we learn to think. We need to do this according to our own motivation rather than someone else's.

The effects of not getting enough time, information and stroking can be seen in our bodies. Usually we have a tightness and stiffness at the base of our necks. Our necks are locked in an attempt to block more sensory experiences until we have properly integrated the ones already inside. Some of us are oozing energy, while others are "not very together". We may have little energy available except in tight, precise sequences. Attempts to control energy in this way can lead to weight problems. We become overweight or underweight. We eat too much or too little. We have constipation or diarrhea.

Solving problems stemming from this period of our life means getting enough time, information and strokes to maintain the process of integration. We must be allowed to experience our own motivation to think, to conceptualize, to find out what we can and cannot control in each situation and to decide on behavior accordingly. Getting protection means feeling safe enough to think about *all* experiences in order to integrate them so that we don't have to sacrifice this need in order to get strokes. Protection at this stage helps us keep sensory input at a level we can handle.

Summary

Ego state:	Adult
Developmental age:	Eighteen months to three years
Activity:	Thinking
Functional metaphor:	Computer
Psychoanalytic equivalent:	Anal
Needs:	Time and information, reasons, limits, affection
Key concepts:	Separateness, contrariness, compliance or rebellion, control issues, shame, pushing, thinking, resistance, integrating, messiness and tidiness
Common body problems:	Uncontrollable discharges of energy, seizures, constipation, diarrhea, stiff neck, central and autonomic nervous systems not together
Problem-solving procedure:	Try and make me
Games and positions:	Schlemiel, stupid, goody-two-shoes, balance sheet, look what you made me do, sunny side up, tell me this, I'll show them
Mechanism:	Discounting
Injunctions, set-ups:	Don't think, don't have needs separate from me, everything is okay with me (no way to have separate positions)

Messages in support of
Thinking:

It's okay for you to push and test, to find limits, to say "No" and become separate from me. You can think for yourself; you don't have to take care of other people by thinking for them. You can be sure about what you need. You can think about your feelings and feel about your thinking. You can let people know when you feel angry. I'm glad you're growing up!

Activities for Thinking

1. I know when I need to develop and use my capacity to think because I:

   _____ push against others

   _____ want my own position

   _____ oppose what's going on

   _____ become preoccupied with "mine and yours" instead of "ours"

   _____ feel stubborn

   _____ act rebellious or compliant

   _____ want to say "no" or "I won't"

2. When I imagine myself in my life now having the freedom, safety and affection I need to think for myself, the following scene comes to mind:

   _____

   _____

   _____

   _____

3. When I picture the two-year old I once was who is still an active, vital part of my life I feel:

_____ scared, _____ sad, _____ happy, _____ joyous,

_____ depressed, _____ enraged, _____ panicked

other _____

4. What the two-year-old I once was needs to know and hear right now is:

_____

_____

5. I will give and receive messages in support of *Thinking* to myself and others in the following ways:

_____

_____

_____

_____

STAGE FOUR

IDENTITY

The SuperNatural Child

(Three to Six Years)

Make love to the demon.
Chogyam Trungpa

When we are stuck in problems stemming from the ages of around three to six years old, we often look like we are going crazy or are possessed by the devil. Some of us seem to have an evil quality about us; others act sinister, frightening or powerful. Some of us look weak, like we are going to fall apart at any moment.

We may seem bent on getting our friends to fight with each other. We often report waking with fright from a nightmare. We are actively involved in magical acts — thinking certain thoughts in order to produce certain effects. We report feeling that we have caused events to happen, no matter how unrelated to our actions those events seem to other people.

Transactions initiated towards us are not likely to be taken "straight". We may respond to a caring remark with hurt, or to a happy story with pain and sorrow. For this reason it does not seem possible to talk with us about what is going on until after it has taken place. Meanwhile, others hold on to their faith that "we know what we need to do". They assume that somehow we must be doing what we need to do, and that somewhere inside us we know how to respond.

These events are directly related to the birth and development of a new capacity and part of our personality — the Parent in the Child, often called the electrode, the witch mother or the troll father. The capacity born at this age works like a transformer capable of changing energy from one form to another. We can turn caring into hurting, joy into sorrow, anger into fear or terror into rage. The fact that we may feel that we do not possess this power is part of the illusion. We all are powerful, creative beings.

This unlikely process is the one by which we are throwing off the effect of all the illusions we internalize about who we really are. Our entire collection of illusions about ourselves and others seems to be contained in this ego state much like a library filled with books. In order to "clean out the shelves" we must direct energy through, or "energize" each illusion or image in order to be done with it. We pull the old skeletons out of the closet and try them on like costumes.

The process is more difficult to complete if those around

us are "taken in" or caught up in the illusion, reinforcing and validating it as if it were our real selves, rather than a costume. We need to hear that we can act like an ogre and even succeed in frightening people, but we are not basically or intrinsically an ogre.

The more "skeletons" we drag out of the closet, try on and discard, the more we can function in this ego state. The nickname "SuperNatural Child" is used because this part of us is the channel through which we get in touch with other than known forces of nature. How we set our channels is called our "script decision".[13] Getting rid of the "skeletons" we open the channel to knowledge of other planes of consciousness. The more open we become, the more we can use our greater intuitive power.

The following guidelines aid the process. The first and most important is "nobody can do it for you". No matter how strong others urge to help you, to point a better way, ultimately, we must each discover for ourselves through our own experience what is valid for us.

Second, outward appearances notwithstanding, "every-body is Buddha"; every one of us is innately okay and powerful. Some of us are simply more convincing actors than others.

Third, people at every age, but especially at this one, are best served by compassionate and total honesty from others — straight reactions to events. This means we all must shed as rapidly as possible our illusions about what we are "supposed to be like" or how we are "supposed to react" or about what is "normal" and what is not. We can even joke about how we don't look like the "Average Human Being" kept locked in a vault in the Bureau of Standards in Washington, D.C., right next to the "Standard Bowel Movement".

While working through problems from this ego state, we report feeling many changes in our physical energy. As we gradually let go of former controls on our energy, our consciousness seems to float on a stormy sea of energy like a tempest. As time passes, our energy finds its own level and the storm subsides. Meanwhile, we are quite susceptible to various illnesses, especially infections and accidents. For that reason it is especially important not to stress relationships with demands for change, but to offer and receive a lot of physical stroking while the adjustments make themselves.

Sometimes we may feel pain over the heart and in our chest muscles. As the "electrode activity" begins to settle down, we feel our chest open up. Behaviorally, we are becoming free to love, to care and to "have a heart".

Summary

Ego state:	SuperNatural Child
Developmental age:	Three to six years
Activity:	Transforming energy
Functional metaphor:	Transformer
Psychoanalytic equivalent:	Genital
Needs:	Adequate external supply lines maintained while testing power
Key concepts:	Magic, potency/impotency, power, caring/hurting, genital orientation, going crazy/ going sane, setting up fights, transformer, electrode, channel
Common body problems:	Circulatory problems, chest pain, palpitations, muscular binding in chest, raised or lowered basal metabolic rate
Problem-solving procedures:	Let's pretend
Games and positions:	Mine's bigger than yours; let's you and him fight; uproar; rapo; cops and robbers; buzz off, buster; let's pull a fast one on Joey; I'm only trying to help

Mechanism: Conversion (repressing an
                              emotion that manifests in a
                              physical symptom)

Injunctions, set-ups: Eat your heart out, don't be
                              sane, don't be powerful,
                              don't be loving, watch out!

Messages in support of   It's okay for you to have your
Identity: own view of the world, to be
                              who you are and to test your
                              power. You can be powerful
                              and still have needs. You
                              don't have to act scary, sick,
                              sad or mad to get taken care
                              of. It's okay for you to ex-
                              plore who you are. It's im-
                              portant for you to find out
                              what you are about. It's okay
                              to imagine things without
                              being afraid you will make
                              them come true. It's okay for
                              you to find out the conse-
                              quences of your own behav-
                              ior.

Activities for Stage Four

1. I know when I need to develop my identity further
   because I:

   _____ am fascinated with dif-   _____ focus on how much I
         ferences   can affect others

   _____ have frequent scary   _____ experiment with differ-
         dreams   ent images of myself

   _____ deal with who I am,
         who others think I am,
         who I thought I was
         and who I can become

2. When I imagine myself in my life now having the freedom, safety and affection I need to explore who I am, the following scene comes to mind:

_____

_____

_____

_____

3. When I picture the preschooler I once was who is still an active, vital part of my life, I feel:

_____ scared, _____ sad, _____ happy, _____ joyous,

_____ depressed, _____ enraged, _____ panicked

other _____

4. What the preschooler I once was needs to know and hear right now is:

_____

_____

5. I will give and receive messages in support of *Identity* to myself and others in the following ways:

_____

_____

_____

_____

STAGE FIVE

SKILLFULNESS

The Parent Ego State
(Six to Twelve Years)

Do it!

Jerry Rubin

When we work through problems from the ages of six to twelve, we often appear to be reverting to two-year-old behavior. We look sullen, sulky, diffident. We feel stuck and confused again. Attempts by others to help us get unstuck are useless — nothing works, again!

As we begin to put words to these events, we can see that nothing others can offer will work because we are getting ready to have our *own* way of doing things, our own Parent ego state. Our "stuckness" says, "I am going to do it my way this time, or not at all!"

We may assume that it is dangerous to let anyone know that we want to have our own way of doing things. Therefore, a first step in problem-solving is finding out that we can disagree with others' ways with no risk to their stability. The next step is putting together our own ways of doing things. For this purpose we need many experiences of doing things our own way, and we need to argue and hassle with others about their ways.

Those of us who took on others' ways instead of creating our own were set up to suffer around doing things because no one else's way exactly fits our nature. We may feel rigid, stiff and inflexible in our bodies and our lifestyles. We may spend a lot of energy trying to please others or getting others to please us. We may experience life as one horrendous experiment being conducted upon us by some mad scientist.

If we can only figure out the formula, we'll be able to run through the maze to our great experimental reward. We get more exhausted than depressed because we've engaged in frantic spurts of activity searching for the "key" or the "secret". Many of us in our adult lives have joined group after group of people who claim to know "the secret". Frequently this has cost us our health and, more often than not, our wealth.

The idea that it might be *fun* to do things, or even that it is *possible* to learn to do things, let alone have fun in the process, is inconceivable. If learning has always been full of pain, we believe there are too many trials and tribulations along its road. Life is serious after all, not something to play around with or make light of. "Tow the line! Knuckle under!

Concentrate! Push!" But our Child has not been blinded to other possibilities. After all, there really *are* people who are contented, for whom things are relatively painless, pleasant and satisfying. There *are* a few competent souls.

To learn how to do things our own way we need to take in new Parent structures in place of the pain and hassle of others. We need to let go of old ways of doing things based on somebody else's way, and find our own way, based on our own needs. The Parent ego state belongs to us, not to some external authority. We need to design it to serve our own internal Child. The machine is built to serve the person, not vice versa. This simple fact may be a revelation: We have built part of our personality upside down.

Next, we will need to replace other structures. We find that looking at anything in terms of good and bad, or making mistakes, or right or wrong, is not problem-solving at all. We simply have to deal with what works.

Then we need to get our personal technology together. How are we going to get our needs met? We need to know how to be angry with a friend and resolve it or with a stranger and resolve it, and how to express fear in such a way as to get reassurance. Then there is the big issue of stroke supply. How can we get strokes? When is it okay, and not okay? Can boys stroke girls, can women stroke men, can people of the same sex stroke each other and under what circumstances? We may need protection while we explore our sexuality with another person of the same sex. We can't learn what being male is all about from females, and likewise women can't learn about being female from men. We need protection to experiment in these relationships without reinforcing the idea that sexuality is not okay or is dangerous.

What will increase the odds of getting the responses we want in our relationships with others? How can two people have needs and feelings at the same time, and both get their needs met? And money — is it all right to have money or not to have money? How much money should we have? What are the right ways to get, keep and spend it? What ways of doing things do others find oppressive? What about caring? Can we care for each other without having to sell each other's souls in the process? How do we relate to power? Is it all right to have power over people?

We discover what will work for us by what we disagree with. Each person's behavior, tic or grimace becomes open to scrutiny. We want enough time now to think about things carefully before we make ideas our own.

The process of letting go of an old structure and taking in a new one requires us to be active. We need to try out the new way, reconsider it, alter it a bit, consult about it, and then repeat it many more times until it becomes an automatic part of us.

Frequently we need to do things to let go of a reservoir of psychic energy which had been stopped up by having to run against someone else's gates. Physical activity often opens blocks, especially the painful place between the shoulder blades where we have been allowing the "monkey on our back" to ride. Our posture improves. Many of us discover that because we were unable to argue with people of the opposite sex, we had unwittingly incorporated the opposite sex structures into our Parent. We feel that something is wrong with us as sexual beings and that we are unlike others of our sex. Our opposite-sex ways make our physical appearances odd, as if trying to look nonchalant while wearing mother's or father's clothes.

As we build up our own technological wardrobe, we gain more control until finally we are able to energize our full power at will, signaling the birth of the last component of our personality structure — our separate Parent ego state. It is the voice of our authority — confident, powerful and completely ours.

We experience enough protection to give birth to our own Parent when we are able to examine many ways of doing things, when we are able to choose our own way and let others know what it is without any cost to our stroke supply or integrity, and when we are able to continue structuring without having to structure for other people against our will.

Summary

Ego state:	Parent
Developmental age:	Six to twelve years
Activity:	Structuring, developing skills
Functional metaphor:	Regulator
Psychoanalytic equivalent:	Latency
Needs:	Experiences in doing things, hassling to incorporate structures
Key concepts:	Doing or not doing things, independence, disagreeing, hassling, arguing, suffering around doing things, latent homosexuality, incorporating structures, making not okay, excluding sex-role behaviors
Common body problems:	Opposite sex distribution of fatty tissue, muscular binding in chest area
Problem-solving procedure:	Dress up
Games and positions:	Courtroom; ain't it awful; blemish; PTA; NIGYSOB (Now I got you, you SOB); kick me
Mechanism:	Exclusion
Injunctions, set-ups:	Don't think, just do it; don't structure; don't exclude; don't make mistakes
Messages in support of *Skillfulness*:	It's okay for you to learn how to do things your own way, to have your own morals and methods. You don't have to suffer to get what you need.

Trust your feelings to guide
you. You can think before
you make that your way. It's
okay to disagree. You can do
it your way.

Activities for Stage Five

1. I know in the following ways when I am developing my
   ability to structure and become skillful because I:

   _____ argue with others   _____ defend against advice

   _____ experience a negative   _____ make others' ways not
         attitude   okay

   _____ become preoccupied   _____ question my own/
         with how things work   others' morals and
                                          values

   _____ feel stubborn

2. When I imagine myself in my life now having the
   freedom, safety and affection to develop my own ways
   and skills, the following scene comes to mind:

   _____

   _____

   _____

   _____

3. When I picture the six- to twelve-year-old child I once
   was who is still an active vital part of my life, I feel:

   _____ scared,   _____ sad,   _____ happy,   _____ joyous,

   _____ depressed,   _____ enraged,   _____ panicked

   other _____

4. What that child I once was needs to know and hear right now is:

_____

_____

5. I will give and receive new messages about *Skillfulness* to myself and others in the following ways:

_____

_____

_____

_____

STAGE SIX

REGENERATION

The Adolescent
(Thirteen to Nineteen Years)

It's neat to be grown-up!
Mac Hawley

73

At around thirteen, we begin a rebirth. We start to regenerate, to pass through our previous stages as we finalize growing up. We begin all of the stages of development over again. We eat all the time; we want to be fed, taken care of, thought *for*. We have high stroking needs. We are concerned about money as an energy supply, and we spend a lot of time talking about sex. We have an incredibly short attention span and are overcome by waves of energy filled with strange, unfamiliar urges — erotic, exciting and scary. We need to have our external supply needs met — we need to be fed and taken care of in a loving way.

We also revisit our exploratory stage around this time. We want periods of time in which to feed our senses, move, touch, smell, hear, see and taste the world again.

At around fourteen we may be stubborn, negative, compliant or rebellious, depending on our mood. We may be messy. We say, "I forgot . . ." as the bathtub overflows into the downstairs. We are testing control and establishing a thinking position in the social world.

At age fifteen we revisit our identity stage. We become preoccupied with who we are, and who we are in relation to others. We test our power to affect other people and experiment with many images, both positive and negative, about who we are and who we can become.

At sixteen we want to argue and hassle. We try to figure out ways not to do something the way others want us to do it. We are getting ready for a friendly divorce from our guardians.

Finally, we want to emerge from our parenting relationship as separate, complete and whole. We want to relate to our guardians as two whole people. We still may need protection, and we definitely still have needs, but we are ready to get these needs met from the larger world. We have assumed responsibility for our own needs, our own feelings, and our own behavior as grown-up people in the world.

Those of us whose scripts say, "Don't grow up," may feel that our emerging sexuality is the worst trauma that could possibly befall us. "Oh no! The one thing that's never supposed to happen is happening! I'm becoming sexual!"

We try various means to compensate. We may wear loose, sloppy clothing to hide our body outlines or we may always look prim, proper and tidy. We may be more than willing to be straight in nurturing others, but not in relating to them sexually. We fear being honest about how we feel because we are ashamed of our sexuality. We expect to lose the stroking and protection we need if we let people know we are experiencing sexual feelings.

Those of us whose scripts say, "Hurry and grow up!" may try to use our emerging sexuality to get our dependency needs met. We are likely to tell sexual jokes, comment on our latest sexual event (fantasy or reality), and act blatantly seductive. We have no time for nurturing. We're looking for some "real action, honey!"

Our sexual encounters are ill-fated because they are angry grown-up attempts to meet the needs of a frightened, helpless child. We may band together in tight, protective cliques to attempt to force what we need from the world.

When we take the position that "even adolescent problems can be solved, even those of us old enough to be sexual can get our needs met", we can clarify what those needs really are. We need to share our feelings and gather information about being sexual beings in a sexual world. We need to know how others experience their sexuality and what they do about it. We must learn how to begin and maintain sexual relationships. We need to learn how to handle the possibilities of pregnancy and venereal disease. And we need to learn how to say no to sexual invitations and still be okay.

Summary

Ego state:	Recycling through previous stages
Developmental age:	13 through 18 years
Activity:	Unifying previous activities
Functional metaphor:	Integrator, pre-flight
Psychoanalytic equivalent:	Puberty

Needs:	Work through previously unsolved problems, sex information and experiences
Key concepts:	Sexuality, recycling of previous stages, unifying functions, integrating personal identity, using cultural parent, breaking family rules
Common body problems:	Delay in sexual development; involutional depressive reactions, both male and female; acne
Problem-solving procedure:	Primary game from each previous stage exaggerated
Mechanism:	Unification
Injunctions, set-ups:	Don't make it; don't grow up
Messages in support of *Regeneration:*	It's okay for you to be sexual, to have a place among the grown-ups and to succeed. You can be a sexual person and still have needs. It's okay to be responsible for your own needs, feelings and behavior. It's okay to be on your own. You're welcome to come home again. My love goes with you.

Activities for Stage Six

1. I know I am revisiting my adolescent stage of development when I:

   _____ feel little and all grown-up at the same time
   _____ want to be on my own/need to be taken care of
   _____ experience many different stages in rapid succession

_____ am preoccupied with sexuality
_____ develop my own personal philosophy
_____ experience turbulent physical changes, often including
acne

2. When I imagine myself in my life now having the freedom, safety and affection I need to deal with my adolescent needs, the following scene comes to mind:

_____
_____
_____
_____

3. When I picture the adolescent I once was who is still an active, vital part of my life, I feel:

_____ scared, _____ sad, _____ happy, _____ joyous,

_____ depressed, _____ enraged, _____ panicked

other _____

4. What the adolescent I once was needs to know and hear right now is:

_____
_____

5. I will give and receive messages in support of *Regeneration* to myself and others in the following ways:

_____
_____
_____
_____

NATURE'S GIFT

The Power Of Recycling

*Things change, then come back to their begin-
nings. Like the circle of the sun and moon, the sky,
the bodies of people and animals, the nests of
birds, the days and seasons — all come back in a
circle. The young grow old and from the old the
young begin and grow. It is the Great Spirit's way.*

Sacajawea *by Anna Lee Waldo*

Drawing a circle, we move the pen in a curve until we return to the place where we began. So, too, do the planets move in orbit, returning to the place from which they started. The earth takes one year to make this journey. Our moon takes only twenty-eight days to accomplish its return. We mark the stages of our developmental cycle as naturally as the daily repetitions of the hours on a clock. In everything and everyone, this cyclical development is nature's design.

However, we may experience our natural return through the stages we began in childhood as abnormal for a number of reasons. We may be accustomed to thinking about life as a linear progression in which there is no return. We may have been encouraged to "put away the things of childhood" and thus have been prevented from experiencing as adults our continuing childlike nature in the unending repetition of stages.

Further, we may have attempted to deal with negative limitations assumed in earlier stages by refusing to allow any space at all for that which vaguely resembled the process of childhood. Ineffective as it may have been, it was one way to cope.

A better alternative would be to use the cycle to finish actively with limited views which are alien to our needs and which cause us pain. We really can open ourselves to greater realities in the service of our needs. We can choose peace and joy over pain and suffering.

Ancient wisdom reminds us that those who forget the past are condemned to repeat it. Using the process of transformation to become free of scripts is indeed a lofty goal. It means being free to pursue our own dreams, instead of somebody else's illusions.

In this book we have examined and worked with all six stages of life. This Cycle of Development is the fertile ground nature provides each of us in which to sow the seeds of our life's dreams and aspirations. As we repeat the stages throughout life, we can be done with negative programming, meet our needs and build advanced skills from basic ones in the same way we build walking skills from the ability to crawl.

We will repeat the stages in the cycle whether or not we choose to use them to accomplish our purposes. If we choose not to use them, we will merely repeat the past with all its limiting familiarity. If we choose to use the cycle to create the results we want in life, we enter into the vast, endless process of growth, sharing the creative potential of the universe, which is our birthright.

With this great understanding of the end and the beginning, and of how the six stages are accomplished, each according to its own time, (the Sage) mounts them as though they were six dragons, and heads for heaven.

I-Ching, Book of Changes
Tuan-chuan

GLOSSARY

ADAPTED. A fixed pattern of behavior designed to please others or one's own internal Parent.

ARCHAIC. Old, arising from an earlier stage of development, often in childhood.

AUTONOMOUS. Self-governing.

CONTAMINATION. The clouding of a present experience by an unintegrated past experience so that what happens now is felt to be the same as the past event.

CONTRACT. A legal, mutual agreement entered into by two or more competent parties; a vehicle through which we give and receive protection.

COUNTERSCRIPT. A collection of messages which can temporarily neutralize destructive script messages.

DISCOUNT. To refuse to take into account, to devalue, especially through not recognizing a person or a problem, and not acknowledging the problem's importance, ability to solve it or the fact it can be solved.

EGO STATE. State of the self when transacting. Named Parent, Adult and Child by Eric Berne, they are the foundation for analyzing transactions.

ESCALATE. To increase the energy in a feeling or problem until it is out of proportion.

GAME. A series of ulterior transactions beginning with a discount, followed by a switch in roles and ending with a payoff that justifies, rather than solves, a problem.

MANIPULATION. To manage or influence by artful or devious skill; to change to suit one's purpose or advantage.

NEED. Something essential to the healthy life and growth of a person, as in "babies *need* touching", "people *need* food and strokes". Also that which is necessary according to the stage of development.

PROBLEM SOLVING. The process of finding solutions for problems or conflicts.

PROTECTION. Setting up situations for safety, first by preventing trouble whenever possible and then by having effective ways of dealing with problems when they arise.

PSYCHIC ENERGY. The energy of the human soul or mind.

REGRESSION. The process of returning to earlier stages of development, using only the physical, mental and emotional systems then available in order to resolve developmental problems.

REPARENTING. The use of regression to replace early parental programs with new and healthy parental experiences.

REPROGRAMMING. The process of transforming an archaic ego state or program.

RESISTANCE. To fight against or withstand the effect of; a way of protecting oneself from an experience one feels is threatening.

SCRIPT. An unconscious life plan based on decisions made during childhood and reinforced by parents, like the written text of a play.

STAGE. A stable portion of the developmental cycle having its own needs, processes and distinctive characteristics. Also, a scene of action in the cycle of life; the platform upon which the primal theater of life is enacted.

STRAIGHT. Relating directly, without ulterior motives; in contrast to *games*.

STROKE. A unit of recognition such as touch, a greeting or a kick.

STRUCTURE. Organized elements of experience constructed to serve as models for doing things.

SUSTAINING SYSTEMS. Those body systems without which life cannot continue, e.g. respiratory, digestive, circulatory, eliminative, immunological.

SYMBIOSIS. A transactional relationship which is characterized by sharing of the functions of feeling, thinking and doing between two or more people.

TRANSACTION. An exchange of strokes consisting of a stimulus from one person and a response from another.

TRANSACTIONAL ANALYSIS. A system of social psychiatry that provides methods of identifying what goes on between people; a form of psychotherapy; a complete theory of personality.

TRANSFORMATION. Reprogramming past, painful experiences, replacing them with new, constructive ones.

TRAUMA. A startling experience that has a lasting effect on mental life.

REFERENCES

1. Berne, Eric. **Transactional Analysis in Psychotherapy.** Grove Press, New York, 1961.

2. For further information on stroking, an excellent book is Montagu, Ashley. **Touching.** Harper & Row, New York, 1971.

3. A thorough work on games is contained in Berne, Eric. **Games People Play.** Grove Press, New York, 1971.

4. Schiff, Aaron Wolfe and Schiff, Jacqui. "Passivity," *Transactional Analysis Journal,* Vol. 1, No. 1, pp. 78-89, January, 1971.

5. See: Steiner, Claude. **Games Alcoholics Play.** Grove Press, and Berne, Eric. **What Do You Say After You Say Hello?**

6. Dass, Ram. **Be Here Now.** Lama Foundation, San Cristobal, New Mexico, 1971, Year of the Monkey.

7. Levin, Pamela. "Think Structure For Feeling Fine Faster," *Transactional Analysis Journal,* Vol. 3, No. 1, pp. 38-39, January, 1973.

8. Crossman, Patricia. "Permission and Protection," *Transactional Analysis Journal,* Vol. 5, No. 19, July, 1966.

9. Berne, Eric. **Principles of Group Treatment.** Oxford University Press, New York, 1966.

10. For another view of programming and reprogramming experiences, see: Lilly, John. **The Center of the Cyclone.** Julian Press, Inc., New York, 1972.

11. The relationship of the stress mechanism to exploratory dynamics was pointed out by Cass, RN, Gracia and Cass, Paul.

12. Karpman, Stephen. "Options," *Transactional Analysis Journal,* Vol. 1, No. 1, pp. 79-87, January, 1971.

13. Goulding, Robert. "New Directions in Transactional Analysis: Creating an Environment for Redecision and Change," a chapter in **Progress in Group and Family Therapy.** Brunner/Mazel, 1972.

RESOURCES

1. To find out how you set your stage to form your own unique developmental design, see: **How to Develop Your Personal Powers**, Pamela Levin, 1982. The book takes you through a series of questions, the answers to which are used to fill in blanks. The result is one sentence describing your dynamic and an affirmation specifically designed to being reprogramming for each stage.

2. For a complete guide to the Cycle of Development and the stages, see: **Cycles of Power, A User's Guide To the Seven Seasons of Life**, Pamela Levin, 1988 (Health Communications, Inc.). The book presents the cycle, the timing of repetitions, stories of people growing through each stage, and tasks we can do to develop each power. Also discussed are body language, cycle sabotage, and reclaiming power in each stage.

3. For a guide to raising children using a parenting model based on the Development Cycle and affirmations for each stage, see: **Self-Esteem: A Family Affair**, by Jean Clarke, Winston Press, Minneapolis, MN, 1978.

4. **The International Transactional Analysis Association** provides a directory of study groups, seminars, and members in good standing. To obtain information and services which meet professional training standards, contact: ITAA, 1772 Vallejo St., San Francisco, CA 94123, (415) 885-5992.

5. **The Experiencing Enough Training** is structured as an intensive experiential training designed for people who want to reclaim the base of abundance that is their birthright. Participants challenge the personal limitations, which result in scarcity by confronting and resolving issues from the first stages of life — conception through age two. For information contact: Conference Coordinator, Experiencing Enough, 3712 - 25th Avenue South, Seattle, WA 98144; (206) 725-7573.

ABOUT THE AUTHOR

Pamela Levin, R.N., is a Clinical Teaching Member of the International Transactional Analysis Association. She conducts a private practice in Northern California. She trained with Eric Berne, founder of Transactional Analysis, and has been active in the Transactional Analysis movement since 1966. She is the author of three books and numerous professional articles. She works with individuals and leads groups, and conducts personal growth and professional training workshops internationally. She is committed to nurturing healthy development at every stage of life and to societal change through people regaining and developing personal power.

She is the first Registered Nurse to be granted Clinical and Clinical Teaching Membership in the International Transactional Analysis Association.

For her work on the Developmental Cycle, the theory of childhood stages repeated throughout adulthood, as presented in her book, *Cycles of Power,* Pamela received the Eric Berne Memorial Scientific Award in 1984.

AFFIRMATIONS

Affirmations for BEING

It's okay for you to be here, to be fed, touched and taken care of.

- You have a right to be here.
- Your needs are okay with me.
- I'm glad you're a (boy/girl).
- You don't have to hurry; you can take your time.
- I like to hold you, to be near you and to touch you.

These messages are important for everybody starting at birth to 6 months; and after that for early teenagers; for people who are ill, tired, hurt or vulnerable; and for everyone else.

Affirmations for DOING THINGS

It's okay for you to move out in the world, to explore, to feed your senses and to be taken care of.

- You can get attention or approval and still act the way you really feel.
- You can do things and get support at the same time.
- It's okay to explore and experiment.
- It's okay for you to initiate.
- You can be curious and intuitive.

These messages are important for everybody starting from 6 to 18 months and also for 13- to 14-year-olds; for people starting a new job, a new relationship, learning a new skill; and for everyone else.

Affirmations for THINKING

It's okay for you to push and test, to find out limits, to say no and to become separate from me.

- I'm glad you're growing up.
- You can let people know when you feel angry.
- You can think about your feelings, and you can feel about your thinking.
- You can think for yourself . . . you don't have to take care of other people by thinking for them.
- You don't have to be uncertain; you can be sure about what you need.

These messages are important for everybody starting at 18 months to 3 years of age and also for middle teens; for everyone who does cause and effect thinking, who is becoming independent, who is developing a new personal position; and for everyone else.

Affirmations for POWER AND IDENTITY

It's okay for you to have your own view of the world, to be who you are and to test your power.

- You can be powerful and still have needs.
- You don't have to act scary, sick, sad or mad to get taken care of.
- It's okay for you to explore who you are. It's important for you to find out what you're about.
- It's okay to imagine things without being afraid you'll make them come true.
- It's okay to find out the consequences of your behavior.

These messages are important for 3- to 6-year-olds, for teenagers, for people owning their own power, for people changing identity, and for everyone else.

Affirmations for STRUCTURE

It's okay for you to learn how to do things your own way, to have your own morals and methods.

- You can think before you make that your way.
- Trust your feelings to guide you.

- You can do it your own way.
- You don't have to suffer to get what you need.
- It's okay to disagree.

These messages are important for 6- to 12-year-olds, for people in their late teens and early 20s, for people entering new social settings, for people learning new ways of doing things, for those changing values and for everyone else.

Affirmations for SEXUALITY AND SEPARATING

It's okay for you to be sexual, to have a place among grown-ups and to succeed.

- You can be a sexual person and still have needs.
- It's okay to be responsible for your own needs, feelings and behavior.
- It's okay to be on your own.
- You're welcome to come home again.
- My love goes with you.

These messages are important for 13- to 19-year-olds; for those pulling up roots, making relationship separations and being a sexual person; and for everyone else.

Cycles of Power © 1988, *Becoming the Way We Are* © 1974, and *How To Develop Your Personal Powers* © 1982 by Pamela Levin.

© Pamela Levin 1987

NOTES

NOTES

NOTES

NOTES

NOTES

A Note from the Author

These affirmation cards are included to provide additional support in achieving your own personal goals in life by providing emotional nutrients needed in each stage of the growth cycle.

Use the cards in various ways. For example:

1. Choose a message randomly.
2. Choose all the messages in the stage most relevant in your life now and use only those until you have them as reality.
3. Ask someone else to choose for you and have them say the message to you.
4. Hide different message cards in various locations where they will surprise you throughout the day.
5. Put them on a plate in your kitchen and choose healthy messages instead of a cookie.
6. Give an appropriate message to a friend in need.

Feel free to invent other ways that will help you seed your mind with this new message so that it can take root and blossom in your life. Refer to the stages in this book to help you dissolve blocks and resistance to the messages.

To obtain additional copies of these affirmation messages (color-coded and laminated circles) for yourself or for gifts, contact: Affirmation Enterprises, P.O. Box 21, Savage, MN 55378.

BEING

You have a right to be here.

BEING

You don't have to hurry; you can take your time.

BEING

Your needs are okay with me.

BEING

I like to hold you, to be near you and to touch you.

BEING

I'm glad you're a (boy/girl).

These messages are important for everybody starting at birth to 6 months; and after that for early teenagers; for people who are ill, tired, hurt and vulnerable; and for everyone else.

From *Becoming The Way We Are*
© 1988
by Pamela Levin
Health Communications, Inc.

From *Becoming The Way We Are*
© 1988
by Pamela Levin
Health Communications, Inc.

From *Becoming The Way We Are*
© 1988
by Pamela Levin
Health Communications, Inc.

From *Becoming The Way We Are*
© 1988
by Pamela Levin
Health Communications, Inc.

From *Becoming The Way We Are*
© 1988
by Pamela Levin
Health Communications, Inc.

From *Becoming The Way We Are*
© 1988
by Pamela Levin
Health Communications, Inc.

DOING THINGS

You can get attention or approval and still act the way you really feel.

DOING THINGS

It's okay for you to initiate.

DOING THINGS

You can do things and get support at the same time.

DOING THINGS

You can be curious and intuitive.

DOING THINGS

It's okay to explore and experiment.

These messages are important for everybody starting from 6 to 18 months and also for 13- to 14-year-olds; for people starting a new job, a new relationship, learning a new skill; and for everyone else.

From *Becoming The Way We Are*
© 1988
by Pamela Levin
Health Communications, Inc.

From *Becoming The Way We Are*
© 1988
by Pamela Levin
Health Communications, Inc.

From *Becoming The Way We Are*
© 1988
by Pamela Levin
Health Communications, Inc.

From *Becoming The Way We Are*
© 1988
by Pamela Levin
Health Communications, Inc.

From *Becoming The Way We Are*
© 1988
by Pamela Levin
Health Communications, Inc.

From *Becoming The Way We Are*
© 1988
by Pamela Levin
Health Communications, Inc.

THINKING

I'm glad you're growing up.

THINKING

You can think for yourself . . . you don't have to take care of other people by thinking for them.

THINKING

You can let people know when you feel angry.

THINKING

You don't have to be uncertain; you can be sure about what you need.

THINKING

You can think about your feelings, and you can feel about your thinking.

These messages are important for everybody starting at 18 months to 3 years of age and also for middle teens; for everyone who does cause and effect thinking, who is becoming independent, who is developing a new personal position; and for everyone else.

From *Becoming The Way We Are*
© 1988
by Pamela Levin
Health Communications, Inc.

From *Becoming The Way We Are*
© 1988
by Pamela Levin
Health Communications, Inc.

From *Becoming The Way We Are*
© 1988
by Pamela Levin
Health Communications, Inc.

From *Becoming The Way We Are*
© 1988
by Pamela Levin
Health Communications, Inc.

From *Becoming The Way We Are*
© 1988
by Pamela Levin
Health Communications, Inc.

From *Becoming The Way We Are*
© 1988
by Pamela Levin
Health Communications, Inc.

POWER
AND IDENTITY

You can be powerful and still have needs.

POWER
AND IDENTITY

It's okay to imagine things without being afraid you'll make them come true.

POWER
AND IDENTITY

You don't have to act scary, sick, sad or mad to get taken care of.

POWER
AND IDENTITY

It's okay to find out the consequences of your behavior.

POWER
AND IDENTITY

It's okay for you to explore who you are. It's important for you to find out what you're about.

These messages are important for 3- to 6-year-olds, for teenagers, for people owning their own power, for people changing identity, and for everyone else.

From *Becoming The Way We Are*
© 1988
by Pamela Levin
Health Communications, Inc.

From *Becoming The Way We Are*
© 1988
by Pamela Levin
Health Communications, Inc.

From *Becoming The Way We Are*
© 1988
by Pamela Levin
Health Communications, Inc.

From *Becoming The Way We Are*
© 1988
by Pamela Levin
Health Communications, Inc.

From *Becoming The Way We Are*
© 1988
by Pamela Levin
Health Communications, Inc.

From *Becoming The Way We Are*
© 1988
by Pamela Levin
Health Communications, Inc.

STRUCTURE

You can think before you make that your way.

STRUCTURE

You don't have to suffer to get what you need.

STRUCTURE

Trust your feelings to guide you.

STRUCTURE

It's okay to disagree.

STRUCTURE

You can do it your own way.

These messages are important for 6- to 12-year-olds, for people in their late teens and early 20s, for people entering new social settings, for people learning new ways of doing this, for those changing values and for everyone else.

From *Becoming The Way We Are*
© 1988
by Pamela Levin
Health Communications, Inc.

From *Becoming The Way We Are*
© 1988
by Pamela Levin
Health Communications, Inc.

From *Becoming The Way We Are*
© 1988
by Pamela Levin
Health Communications, Inc.

From *Becoming The Way We Are*
© 1988
by Pamela Levin
Health Communications, Inc.

From *Becoming The Way We Are*
© 1988
by Pamela Levin
Health Communications, Inc.

From *Becoming The Way We Are*
© 1988
by Pamela Levin
Health Communications, Inc.

SEXUALITY
AND
SEPARATING

You can be a sexual person and still have needs.

SEXUALITY
AND
SEPARATING

You're welcome to come home again.

SEXUALITY
AND
SEPARATING

It's okay to be responsible for your own needs, feelings and behavior.

SEXUALITY
AND
SEPARATING

My love goes with you.

SEXUALITY
AND
SEPARATING

It's okay to be on your own.

These messages are important for 13- to 19-year-olds; for those pulling up roots, making relationship separations and being a sexual person; and for everyone else.

From *Becoming The Way We Are*
© 1988
by Pamela Levin
Health Communications, Inc.

From *Becoming The Way We Are*
© 1988
by Pamela Levin
Health Communications, Inc.

From *Becoming The Way We Are*
© 1988
by Pamela Levin
Health Communications, Inc.

From *Becoming The Way We Are*
© 1988
by Pamela Levin
Health Communications, Inc.

From *Becoming The Way We Are*
© 1988
by Pamela Levin
Health Communications, Inc.

From *Becoming The Way We Are*
© 1988
by Pamela Levin
Health Communications, Inc.